COLORADO DESERT
Wildflowers

A GUIDE TO FLOWERING PLANTS OF THE LOW DESERT,
INCLUDING THE COACHELLA VALLEY, ANZA-BORREGO DESERT,
AND PORTIONS OF JOSHUA TREE NATIONAL MONUMENT

D0050426

TEXT AND PHOTOGRAPHS BY
JON MARK STEWART

Text and photography: Jon Mark Stewart

Design: Katey O'Neill and Jon Mark Stewart

Production: John Evarts, Cachuma Press

Chapter opener illustration: Allison Atwill

Printed and bound in Singapore.

Library of Congress Cataloging-in-Publication Data
Stewart, Jon Mark, 1957-
     Colorado Desert Wildflowers: a guide to flowering plants of
the low desert, including the Coachella Valley, Anza-Borrego
Desert, and portions of Joshua Tree National Monument /
text and photographs by Jon Mark Stewart.
        p.   cm.
     Includes index.
     ISBN 0-9634909-0-7 : $12.95
     1. Angiosperm—Colorado Desert (Calif. and Mexico)
2. Wildflowers—Colorado Desert (Calif. and Mexico)   I. Title.
QK149.S68   1992
583.13 ' 09794 ' 99—dc20   92-43056
                                                            CIP

*Front cover: A brilliant display of wildflowers in the Colorado Desert.
Title page: Sand dunes covered by dune marigold and sand verbena.
Back cover: Beavertail cactus in bloom.*

This book is dedicated in memory of my parents, John and Lee, who provided me with the encouragement and the freedom to explore the natural world we live in.

PREFACE

Of the wondrous and sometimes encyclopedic books printed on wildflowers, most can be described as either overwhelming or incomplete. One might even say that any wildflower book that attempts to cover more than one or two square miles can easily become either too large and cumbersome for popular use or too superficial to be called a true guide. Finding the perfect balance between completeness and practicality is a dilemma that has faced every author who has ever attempted to compile a wildflower book.

I admit that this book faced the same challenge, and in response I elected to limit the area covered in the following pages to the Colorado Desert. My goal was to provide the visitor to this wonderful desert with an accurate volume that can be used by beginners and professionals alike to identify some of the more common wildflowers of the Colorado Desert. The reader should understand that the plants listed in these pages barely scratch the surface of the floral diversity found in the Colorado Desert.

The Colorado Desert covers a vast area stretching from the Coachella Valley around Palm Springs, California almost to Phoenix, Arizona, 250 miles eastward. From Needles, California, it extends southward into northern Sonora and Baja California, Mexico. While the emphasis was placed on the low desert region of California, many of the plants illustrated are found in Arizona and Mexico. Some wildflowers found in Joshua Tree National Monument are also included since portions of the Colorado Desert are included within the boundaries of the Monument, and because of its close proximity to the Coachella Valley.

While deserts are often portrayed as barren and lifeless, nothing could be farther from the truth. Within the California portion of the Colorado Desert alone, there are over 800 naturally occurring plants. Of these, only 100 of the most colorful are illustrated here. In walking the fine line between overwhelming and incomplete, I have included some plants that can easily be found by every visitor, as well as less common plants chosen not only for their aesthetic value, but also as a challenge for those who enjoy the excitement of hunting for something new. My hope is that this book will encourage the reader to learn more about the natural world we live in and heighten the visitor's enjoyment of wandering through this magnificent desert region.

To make this book simple to use, plants are arranged by flower color and then botanically within each color. This allows plants that are similar in appearance and color to be grouped together, easing identification. Because cacti are unique, they have been separated into their own group at the back of the book. Common names have come from several sources (including my imagination), but mostly from *Desert Wild Flowers* by Edmund C. Jaeger.

Every attempt has been made to use photographs showing individuals that are typical of the species. Plants of extra large stature or unusual display were avoided. Wildflowers vary in size as the season progresses, so an attempt was made to use plants of average size and condition. Probably the most difficult task was insuring that enough information was presented in the photograph to aid identification.

Scientific terms have been avoided since adequately descriptive English words are readily available. For accuracy, botanical names are included along with the family name. Even though many groups of plants have been revised, this publication follows *A Flora of Southern California* (Munz). This was done to make the book compatible with existing references that may be used for more information.

Books like this are never a solo effort. I would like to thank my wife, Nylia, for her tolerance and encouragement, her patience in the field, and apologize for making her, at times, a "computer widow." Sue Adams, Caroline Kolbert, in addition to those listed below, deserve thanks for proofing the text and preventing me from making major assaults against the English language. My good friends Dexter, Lupita, Rosa, and Spotted Owl deserve a warm thank-you for encouraging me to continue even when spring flowers were scarce. And last, but not least, I would like to thank the rain god who gave me the spring of 1992, for which I am forever grateful.

Jon Mark Stewart
Palm Desert, California
September 1992

CONTENTS

Opposite: Beargrass (Nolina bigelovii)

Opposite: Dune primrose (Oenothera deltoides)

DESERT LILY, AJO LILY
Hesperocallis undulata

Lily Family
Liliaceae

Desert lily is occasionally found in sandy soils of the Colorado Desert. The flowers are fragrant and closely resemble those of the cultivated Easter lily. The desert lily begins blooming in March and can continue blooming into May. It can reach a height of 3 feet (1 m) or more in favorable years. The name ajo lily comes from the Spanish word for garlic, a flavor that Spanish and Native Americans found agreeable. A lily preserve has been set aside near the town of Desert Center.

MOJAVE YUCCA
Yucca schidigera

Agave Family
Agavaceae

A common desert native, Mojave yucca is found throughout the Colorado Desert on well drained soils mostly above 1,000 feet (320 m) elevation. The stringy fibers on the margins of the leaves are characteristic of this plant and distinguish Mojave yucca from the Joshua tree, a tree yucca common in the Mojave Desert and namesake of Joshua Tree National Monument. The fruit was eaten by Native Americans raw, roasted, or ground into meal. The leaf fibers were also used for rope, sandals, and baskets. Mojave yucca can grow to a height of 10 feet (3 m) or taller.

PRICKLY POPPY

Argemone munita ssp. *argentea*

Poppy Family
Papaveraceae

Prickly poppy is found along roadsides, washes, and in other disturbed areas. It grows to about 3 feet (1 m) tall and is covered with prickles on the stems, leaves, and flower buds. The flowers can be 4 to 5 inches (10 to 13 cm) wide, and the stems exude a yellow sap when cut.

WISHBONE BUSH
Mirabilis bigelovii

Four-O'Clock Family
Nyctaginaceae

Wishbone bush is found on rocky slopes and in sandy washes, usually between boulders. The white or sometimes pink flowers are produced in April and May. Its common name alludes to the wishbone type of branching. The leaves are mostly less than 1 inch (25 mm) long. A similar but less common species is white four-o'clock (*Mirabilis tenuiloba*) which has larger leaves (1½ inches, 3 to 4 cm) and is found along the western border of the Colorado Desert.

DEAD-MAN'S FINGERS
Calandrinia ambigua

Purslane Family
Portulacaceae

Dead-man's fingers is also known as desert pot-herb because this plant was used by pioneers and Native Americans for greens. Occasionally found on alkaline slopes and washes, this succulent, green, tufted plant is reported to have a pleasant taste. Look for this plant on the dry barren slopes of the Mecca Hills and in the badlands of Anza-Borrego Desert State Park. The plant grows close to the ground, spreading about 12 inches (30 cm). The flowers are white and very small.

SPECTACLE POD
Dithyrea californica

Mustard Family
Brassicaceae

Spectacle pod is an ephemeral spring wildflower and common member of the sand dune community. The two round, spectacle-shaped fruits are distinctive. Close examination of the flowers will reveal four white petals and six stamens characteristic of the mustard family. Spectacle pod is one of the first wildflowers to bloom on the sand dunes and can be found as early as February. The stems grow to about 12 inches long (30 cm).

WOOLLY PLANTAIN
Plantago insularis

Plantain Family
Plantaginaceae

This very common ephemeral wildflower occurs on bajadas and sandy places, usually in great abundance. The leaves are white, woolly, and clustered at the base of the plant. In good rainfall years, woolly plantain can be quite bushy. The plant is usually less than 5 inches (13 cm) tall. The flower bracts usually have a green mid-rib and the flowers are in a tight spike at the end of a slender stalk.

SMALL-LEAVED AMSONIA
Amsonia brevifolia

Dogbane Family
Apocynaceae

This very attractive shrub is common at mid-elevations in Joshua Tree National Monument and known from scattered mountainous locations in the Colorado Desert. The flowers are white to sky blue. The plant is usually dark green with milky sap, though grayish plants of the variety *tomentosa* coexist with the dark green variety. The plant is very common around Cottonwood Spring in Joshua Tree National Monument and Aztec Well in the Chuckwalla Mountains. Small-leaved amsonia is a shrubby perennial 8 to 16 inches (20 to 40 cm) tall.

DESERT APRICOT
Prunus fremontii

Rose Family
Rosaceae

Common at mid-elevations in the Santa Rosa Mountains, desert apricot is a deciduous shrub 6 feet (2 m) or taller, found on gentle slopes and in washes. The white flowers appear in early spring, usually by the first few weeks of February and as early as January. The flowers can be so dense that the plant seems to lack leaves. The plant gets its common name from the small fruits produced in late spring and early summer, which are not recommended for consumption.

BROWN-EYED PRIMROSE
Camissonia claviformis

Evening Primrose Family
Onagraceae

Brown-eyed primrose is a very common ephemeral in all sandy situations from dunes to washes. The plant is usually less than 12 inches (30 cm) tall. The flowers are white or yellow (see page 42) with a brownish red center, which distinguishes this evening primrose from woody bottle-washer. As the flowers fade, club-shaped fruits are produced. Brown-eyed primrose, like most desert primroses, is a favorite food of the white-lined sphinx moth *(Hyles lineata)*. The caterpillars feed on the leaves and the adult moths feed on the night-blooming flowers.

WOODY BOTTLE-WASHER
Camissonia boothii

Evening Primrose Family
Onagraceae

Woody bottle-washer gets its common name from the wooden stems left behind after the plant dries out. This ephemeral is less than 8 inches (20 cm) tall and is common on bajadas throughout the Colorado Desert. The flowers are clustered more tightly than the brown-eyed primrose and the bottle-washer lacks the brown center.

DUNE PRIMROSE
Oenothera deltoides

Evening Primrose Family
Onagraceae

Dune primrose is a common ephemeral wildflower on sand dunes throughout the Colorado Desert that grows about 1 foot (30 cm) tall; it is also known as bird-cage primrose. The large flowers, 2 to 3 inches (5 to 8 cm) wide, are fragrant and open during the evening, lasting until mid-morning. The plant is pollinated by the white-lined sphinx moth (*Hyles lineata*) which, at first glance, may be confused with a nocturnal hummingbird. As the plant dries out, the stems curl toward the center and produce a characteristic "bird cage."

JIMSON WEED, MOON FLOWER
Datura meteloides

Nightshade Family
Solanaceae

Jimson weed is one of two daturas found in the Colorado Desert. The second is the annual small datura *(Datura discolor)*. The two differ enough to be easily told apart. Small datura is a summer/fall annual with smaller flowers and a smaller stature (20 inches, 50 cm tall). The flowers of small datura also have a purple throat not found in jimson weed. Jimson weed is a larger plant (3 feet, 1 m tall) and is also a short-lived perennial, blooming mostly in the spring, though it can be found blooming almost any time of year. The flowers are very fragrant.

DESERT TOBACCO
Nicotiana trigonophylla

Nightshade Family
Solanaceae

Desert tobacco is a common wildflower found on rocky slopes at lower elevations. The plant is a short-lived perennial or biennial growing to about 1 or 2 feet (30 to 60 cm) tall. The toxic leaves are dark green, very sticky, and ill smelling. Desert tobacco is related to the domestic tobacco, *N. tabacum,* and though very toxic, was smoked by Native Americans during religious ceremonies. A similar plant that occurs in sandy soils is *N. clevelandii.* Desert tobacco differs by having ear-shaped appendages at the base of the leaves.

FORGET-ME-NOTS
Cryptantha sp.

Borage Family
Boraginaceae

Of all the wildflowers found in the Colorado Desert, none are more confusing than the forget-me-nots. About eight species occur in this desert. The forget-me-not illustrated here is the common narrow-leafed forget-me-not (*Cryptantha angustifolia*), which is widespread in sandy soils. The small white flowers are characteristic of this group, though flower and leaf size are variable.

GHOST FLOWER
Mohavea confertiflora

Figwort Family
Scrophulariaceae

A favorite among desert wildflower enthusiasts, ghost flower is found in washes and occasionally on sandy hillsides. Though ghost flower is an ephemeral, in good years the plant can be a small, bushy shrub about 16 inches (40 cm) tall. Inside the silky flowers are lines of maroon spots. The leaves are sticky. While it resembles sand blazing-star (*Mentzelia involucrata*—see page 32), it differs by having the petals united into a cup, unlike blazing-star's five separate petals.

DESERT STAR
Monoptilon bellioides

Sunflower Family
Asteraceae

One of many "belly flowers," desert star is a small prostrate annual found on bajadas. The penny-sized (or smaller) "flowers" have white rays with a yellow center. The plant forms a mat that is usually 4 to 6 inches (10 to 15 cm) across. Desert star is in a group of desert ephemerals affectionately known as "belly flowers" because they are small plants that require admirers to get down on their bellies to enjoy them.

WHITE TIDY-TIPS
Layia glandulosa

White tidy-tips is a common wildflower in the northern Colorado Desert and Joshua Tree National Monument. The plant is a spring ephemeral in sandy soils. The flower heads are white with a yellow center, but the rays can fade with age to rose-purple. The flower heads are a little over an inch wide (3 cm), and the plant is usually about 5 inches (13 cm) tall.

ROCK DAISY
Perityle emoryi

Sunflower Family
Asteraceae

Rock daisy is a common wildflower on rocky slopes and in sandy washes during the spring time. The flower heads are dime size with white rays and a yellow center. The leaves and stems are dark green and almost succulent. Rock daisy can grow to 2 feet (60 cm) tall in good years, but is usually less than 1 foot (30 cm) tall.

FREMONT PINCUSHION
Chaenactis fremontii

Sunflower Family
Asteraceae

Fremont pincushion is one of three common pincushion flowers found in the Colorado Desert. This 4- to 8-inch-tall (10 to 20 cm) plant is found in sandy soils, from blow sand to sandy washes. The flowers are white and the leaves are thinly dissected. The other two pincushion flowers include pebble pincushion (C. *carphoclinia*), which is found on dry bajadas, and Esteve pincushion (C. *stevioides*), which resembles Fremont pincushion but has hairy stems and leaves that are dissected twice instead of once. Esteve pincushion is also found more commonly in the eastern desert.

PARACHUTE PLANT
Atrichoseris platyphylla

Sunflower Family
Asteraceae

A chicory relative, parachute plant is also known as tobacco-weed because the leaves look like those of the tobacco plant. Found in sandy or rocky soils, parachute plant can grow to over 2 feet (60 cm) tall. The leaves lie flat to the ground while the stems rise up and are topped with white flowers with a vanilla-like fragrance. Parachute plant acquired its common name because in good years the plant can become so full of flowers that it appears to be floating in air.

DESERT CHICORY
Rafinesquia neomexicana

Sunflower Family
Asteraceae

Desert chicory is one of many chicory relatives found in the Colorado Desert. Each flower in the composite head is strap shaped and has five teeth on the tip of each strap, resulting from the union of five petals. Desert chicory grows about 18 inches (45 cm) tall and is found in sandy washes by itself or frequently growing up through other shrubs. The white flowers are streaked with purple veins on their backs. Tack-stem (*Calycoseris wrightii*) differs from desert chicory by having small, tack-shaped glands on the stems and leaves that are finely divided and not coursely toothed.

YELLOW FLOWERS

Opposite:Dune marigold (Baileya pleniradiata)

DESERT TRUMPET
Eriogonum inflatum

Buckwheat Family
Polygonaceae

Desert trumpet is a short-lived perennial common to washes and sandy plains. The inflated stems are characteristic and grow 1 to 3 feet (30 to 90 cm) tall. The yellow flowers are only about ¹⁄₁₆ inch (2 mm) long. Plants with uninflated stems are sometimes found, and they are the variety *deflatum*. A similar plant with uninflated stems is Thomas eriogonum (*Eriogonum thomasii*), a spring annual that grows 4 to 8 inches (10 to 20 cm) tall.

LITTLE GOLD POPPY
Eschscholzia minutiflora

Poppy Family
Papaveraceae

A tiny-flowered poppy, little gold poppy occurs in washes and disturbed places throughout the Colorado Desert. While the plant can grow to 1½ feet (45 cm) tall, the petals are only about ¼ inch (6 mm) long.

DESERT POPPY
Eschscholzia parishii

Poppy Family
Papaveraceae

This common little poppy resembles the famous California poppy, but has yellow flowers instead of orange. This plant can be found on rocky slopes and on bajadas. The flower stems grow to 1 foot (30 cm) tall and can either be leafy or naked. Flowering starts in March and continues into April.

PRINCE'S PLUME
Stanleya pinnata

Mustard Family
Brassicaceae

This handsome perennial is occasional in the Santa Rosa Mountains and more common around Joshua Tree National Monument. The flower stalks are present in spring and grow about 5 feet (1½ m) tall. The plant grows mostly in washes and is known to accumulate the poisonous mineral selenium. The stalked fruits of prince's plume are characteristic of the plant and somewhat unusual in the mustard family.

COYOTE MELON
Cucurbita palmata

Gourd Family
Cucurbitaceae

Coyote melon is a trailing plant whose stems can stretch 6 feet (2 m). The flowers are about 2 inches (5 cm) long and are followed by a large yellow gourd 4 inches (10 cm) in diameter. While the common name implies edibility, the plant is not tasty and may be poisonous. The twining stems grow from a tuber that can be several feet across.

BLAZING STAR
Mentzelia sp.

This group of blazing stars is one of the most variable wildflowers in the Colorado Desert. About three or four similar species occur here and telling them apart can be quite difficult. Probably the most common species is M. *albicaulis*, which in itself has variable leaf and flower characteristics. The plant is about 1 foot (30 cm) tall and occurs in sandy places from sand dunes to washes. The group is widespread throughout both the Mojave and Colorado deserts.

SAND BLAZING STAR
Mentzelia involucrata

Stick-Leaf Family
Loasaceae

The five satiny-yellow petals and rough stems and leaves separate this wildflower from ghost flower (see page 17). It is a common spring ephemeral on hot hillsides and flats and occasionally in washes. The flowers are about 1 inch (25 mm) long, growing on stems between 6 and 12 inches (15 to 30 cm) tall.

BLADDER POD

Isomeris arborea

Bladder pod is a common perennial shrub that grows in washes. The plant is about 4 feet (1.2 m) tall and can flower at any time of year, though mostly in the spring. This plant is a favorite nectar plant for hummingbirds and one can almost always be found nearby. The yellow flowers give way to an inflated pod that contains several seeds. This plant is related to the commercial capers.

ROCK DUDLEYA
Dudleya saxosa ssp. *aloides*

Stonecrop Family
Crassulaceae

Rock dudleya is one of two species of live-forevers found in the Colorado Desert. The leaves are 1 to 4 inches (3 to 10 cm) long and about ½ inch (12 mm) wide. The flower stalk can be 8 inches (20 cm) tall with yellow flowers that turn red as they mature. The other, less common species is *D. arizonica*, which has brick red flowers and broad, flat leaves 2 to 6 inches (5 to 15 cm) long and 1 to 2 inches (2 to 5 cm) wide. Rock dudleya is found on rocky hillsides, usually tucked beneath a rock and barely exposed.

CAT'S CLAW ACACIA
Acacia greggii

Also known as "wait-a-minute" bush, cat's claw is a common shrub found in the washes of the Colorado Desert. The plant grows to 6 feet (2 m) or taller, often developing into a small tree. The yellow flowers that appear in April to May grow in a narrow spike and are followed by 4- to 5-inch-long (10 to 13 cm) bean pods. The plant differs from honey mesquite by having a single cat-claw-shaped spine instead of paired straight spines. Another difference is that the mesquite's leaves are twice the size of cat's claw leaves.

DESERT SENNA
Cassia armata

Pea Family
Fabaceae

Desert senna is a nearly leafless shrub about 3 feet (1 m) broad found in
scattered locations in the Colorado Desert, including Chuckwalla Bench,
Chemehuevi Valley, and Anza-Borrego Desert State Park. It is very
common in Joshua Tree National Monument. A relative of desert senna
is Coues' cassia (*C. covesii*). Coues' cassia is a rare plant found in washes.
Unlike desert senna, Coues' cassia is a short-lived perennial less than 10
inches (25 cm) tall and is not shrubby.

BLUE PALO VERDE
Cercidium floridum

Pea Family
Fabaceae

Palo verde, which translates to "green stick," is a common tree up to 30 feet (10 m) tall in washes of the Colorado Desert. This particular species is appropriately named because the bark (except on very old trunks) is blue green. Research has shown that 40% of the tree's annual photosynthesis occurs in the bark. The tree is covered with yellow flowers in spring.

DESERT ROCK-PEA
Lotus rigidus

Pea Family
Fabaceae

A common perennial shrub, desert rock-pea can be found in washes and on rocky hillsides. The flowers are yellow and turn red with age. The plant is somewhat woody, multi-stemmed, and less than 3 feet (90 cm) tall. During the summer, the plant is leafless and appears to be dead, but with winter rains the plant rejuvenates. A similar plant is deer weed (*Lotus scoparius* ssp. *brevialatus*) found in washes of the Santa Rosa Mountains.

PALE PRIMROSE
Camissonia pallida ssp. *hallii*

Evening Primrose Family
Onagraceae

Pale primrose is the only prostrate yellow-flowered primrose in the Colorado Desert. The flowers are small, usually about ½ inch (12 mm) wide, and yellow with one to three red dots near the base of each petal. It grows in dry sandy places and on alluvial fans. This ephemeral sprawls to a diameter of about 5 inches (12 cm).

CALIFORNIA EVENING PRIMROSE
Camissonia californica

Evening Primrose Family
Onagraceae

This evening primrose is common in washes of the Santa Rosa Mountains southward into the mountain ranges of Anza-Borrego Desert State Park. The plant is erect and open branched, usually about 2 feet (60 cm) tall. The flowers are yellow, often with reddish spots near the base, fading to pink with age.

YELLOW CUPS
Camissonia brevipes

Evening Primrose Family
Onagraceae

Yellow cups is a bright, yellow-flowered ephemeral found on dry, stony slopes, bajadas, and occasionally in washes. Most of its leaves are found at the base of the plant, with the flower stalks rising leafless and growing to about 16 inches (40 cm). A similiar plant is heart-leafed primrose (*Camissonia cardiophylla*). The leaves of yellow cups are dissected and lobed instead of heart shaped.

BROWN-EYED PRIMROSE
Camissonia claviformis ssp. *peirsonii*

Evening Primrose Family
Onagraceae

While more commonly white (see page 11), brown-eyed primrose also comes in shades of yellow in the southern Colorado Desert from the Salton Sea to Anza-Borrego Desert State Park. The flowers in this variety are yellow with a brownish-red center, which separates this evening primrose from yellow cups and the several other yellow primroses. This primrose, like all desert primroses, is a favorite food of the white-lined sphinx moth (*Hyles lineata*). The caterpillars feed on the leaves and the adult moths feed on the night-blooming flowers.

CREOSOTE BUSH
Larrea tridentata

Caltrop Family
Zygophyllaceae

Creosote bush is the most common native shrub in the Coachella Valley and probably the Colorado Desert. The plant grows 3 to 6 feet (1 to 2 m) tall. The flowers that appear in spring are followed by fruit that resemble fuzzy balls. Watch the ground and you may find a velvet ant that looks like one of these balls crawling around. The branches may support a green or brown growth the size of a golf ball. This is an insect gall that belongs to the creosote gall midge, a tiny fly that lays its eggs on creosote branches.

THICK-LEAFED GROUNDCHERRY
Physalis crassifolia

Nightshade Family
Solanaceae

Groundcherry is an intricately branched perennial shrub about 1 foot (30 cm) across. It commonly grows on rocky slopes but can also be found in washes. The flowers are yellow and resemble the common tomato, to which it is related. As the fruit ripens, the leafy base of the flower expands to form a lantern over the green berry.

WHISPERING BELLS
Emmenanthe penduliflora

Whispering bells is a delicate spring ephemeral found mostly on rocky slopes and on bajadas. The pale yellow flowers are pendulous and the stems are 4 to 12 inches (10 to 30 cm) tall and covered with white hairs. Whispering bells can be especially common in areas that have recently burned in wildfires.

CHECKER FIDDLENECK
Amsinckia tessellata

Borage Family
Boraginaceae

Checker fiddleneck is a relatively common wildflower in dry sandy or gravelly places, especially in washes. The orange-yellow flowers are arranged into a scorpion-tail-like spike that uncoils as new flowers open. This ephemeral grows to 2 feet (60 cm) and the flowers are ½ inch (12 mm) long. Handling or brushing against this plant should be avoided since the long white hairs can be quite irritating.

DESERT UNICORN
Proboscidea althaeifolia

Martynia Family
Martyniaceae

Desert unicorn is a summer perennial found in sandy places such as washes and roadsides. It is a rare wildflower found in the Vallecito Mountains of Anza-Borrego Desert State Park and around the Chuckwalla Bench. The plant blooms after summer rains and grows to about 1 foot (30 cm) tall. In fall, the plant produces a woody pod about 5 inches (12 cm) long with two curved horns. Native Americans used fibers from the pods in basket making.

DUNE SUNFLOWER
Helianthus niveus ssp. *canescens*

Sunflower Family
Asteraceae

This spring ephemeral is uncommon on sand dunes throughout the Colorado Desert. The plant is usually 2 feet (60 cm) or taller. The flower heads have yellow rays and a red to purple center. The plant is whitish because of hairs that cover the leaves and stems. A rare subspecies, *H. n. tephrodes*, occurs on dune systems between Yuma and the Imperial Valley. It is usually a perennial shrub over 3 feet (1 m) tall.

BRITTLEBUSH, INCIENSO
Encelia farinosa

Sunflower Family
Asteraceae

Brittlebush is a common perennial shrub 1 to 3 feet (30 to 90 cm) tall on rocky hillsides and sandy bajadas. The yellow daisies appear in spring and can brighten hillsides with their mass of flowers. In the eastern desert, brittlebush can have "flowers" with yellow rays but a maroon center and is known as the variety *phenicodonta*. Its leaves are covered with insulating white hairs that reduce water loss. In extreme drought, it loses its leaves to conserve water. The common name incienso (incense in Spanish) comes from the early missionary use of burning the resin for incense.

DESERT SUNFLOWER
Geraea canescens

Sunflower Family
Asteraceae

Desert sunflower is a common ephemeral in sandy soils throughout the Colorado Desert and is capable of broad displays of color. Desert sunflower grows to about 2 feet (60 cm) with flower heads almost 2 inches (5 cm) across. It is frequently found with other dune natives like sand verbena and dune primrose.

LAX-FLOWER
Baileya pauciradiata

Sunflower Family
Asteraceae

Lax-flower is a common ephemeral wildflower on sand dunes throughout the Colorado Desert. The leaves and stems are heavily covered with a white wool. The plant can grow bushy, and though usually smaller, can reach a height of 2 feet (60 cm). The ray flowers are about ¼ inch (6 mm) long and turn downward with age, becoming papery when dry.

ERIOPHYLLUM
Eriophyllum wallacei

Sunflower Family
Asteraceae

This plant is one of the few listed in this book lacking a common name, even though it is plentiful in the desert. It is a "belly flower" because the little woolly tufts grow very low to the ground. The flowers are golden yellow, except along the western edge of the Colorado Desert where plants of the variety *rubellum* can be reddish.

YELLOWHEAD
Trichoptilium incisum

Sunflower Family
Asteraceae

Although quite common, yellowhead is a frequently overlooked ephemeral in sandy places and on desert pavements (flat surfaces of tightly interlocked stones caused by wind and water erosion). The plant is usually small, about 4 inches (10 cm) tall, but in wet years can grow to 8 inches (20 cm). The fragrant leaves are sharp-toothed and white-woolly. Flowers can appear in spring and fall and are yellow in color.

CHINCH WEED
Pectis papposa

Sunflower Family
Asteraceae

Chinch weed is a common fall ephemeral that grows in sandy situations in response to summer rainfall. The yellow daisies can carpet sand dunes in good years. The plant is usually less than 8 to 10 inches (20 to 25 cm) wide, and the foliage is heavily but agreeably scented.

MOJAVE GROUNDSEL
Senecio mohavensis

Sunflower Family
Asteraceae

Mojave groundsel is a small ephemeral occasionally found alongside washes, mostly in shady spots around rocks or trees. The plant is usually less than 6 inches (15 cm) tall, though it can grow to twice that size. The flower heads are yellow and about ¼ inch (6 mm) long in loose clusters.

DESERT VELVET
Psathyrotes ramosissima

Sunflower Family
Asteraceae

Desert velvet is a common wildflower in open places such as hillsides and washes. It is a compact little plant with gray green, velvety leaves and small yellow flowers. Because the plant forms a tight rounded cushion, sometimes 1 foot (30 cm) across, it is also known as "velvet rosette" or "turtle back."

DESERT DANDELION
Malacothrix glabrata

Sunflower Family
Asteraceae

Desert dandelion is a common ephemeral that grows 4 to 12 inches (10 to 30 cm) tall on sandy plains throughout the Colorado Desert. The flowers are light yellow and when young have a red button in the center. The leaves are dissected into many narrow lobes usually clustered at the base. After wet winters, desert dandelion can carpet large areas, outcompeting other wildflowers for attention. Joshua Tree National Monument is well known for its vast displays of desert dandelion.

ORANGE TO RED FLOWERS

Opposite: Chuparosa (Beloperone californica)

DESERT or APRICOT MALLOW
Sphaeralcea ambigua

Mallow Family
Malvaceae

Desert mallow is probably a universal favorite among "desert rats." The apricot to orange flowers are found in spring and in good years can completely cover the plant. The stems and leaves are covered with star-shaped hairs which can be seen with a hand lens or other magnifier. Desert mallow is a perennial shrub to 3 feet (1 m) tall, and grows in washes and on rocky hillsides.

DESERT FUCHSIA
Zauschneria californica ssp. *latifolia*

Evening Primrose Family
Onagraceae

Desert fuchsia is an occasional perennial shrub with stems 4 to 20 inches (10 to 50 cm) long found near seeps and springs in Joshua Tree National Monument, the Santa Rosa and San Jacinto mountains, and southward to the Mexican border. The red tubular flowers are a favorite with hummingbirds. The plant blooms mostly in the fall and can form a mat up to several feet across.

OCOTILLO
Fouquieria splendens

Ocotillo Family
Fouquieriaceae

The usually barren stems, between 6 and 20 feet (2 to 6 m) tall, bear many stout spines which characterize this widespread desert native. While appearing to be a cactus, it is not. The scarlet flowers and bright green leaves appear after rains anytime from spring through fall. Ocotillo is found in rocky, well-drained soils and on dry hillsides. Hummingbirds and orioles are frequently found feeding on the flowers. This plant is legally protected in California and Arizona and may not be collected.

INDIAN PAINTBRUSH
Castilleja chromosa

Figwort Family
Scrophulariaceae

Indian paintbrush occurs in sandy soils in Joshua Tree National Monument and grows to 16 inches (40 cm) tall. The characteristic cluster of red flowers easily identifies this wildflower. It begins blooming in early April and can continue into summer. A similar plant, C. *stenantha*, occurs along streams draining the Santa Rosa and San Jacinto mountains. Both plants are favorites with hummingbirds.

CARDINAL MONKEYFLOWER
Mimulus cardinalus

Figwort Family
Scrophulariaceae

Cardinal monkeyflower is a common wildflower along streams and on seeps in the Santa Rosa and San Jacinto mountains. This scarlet-flowered perennial grows about 1½ feet (45 cm) tall in the desert but can get taller. It regularly occurs with its yellow-flowered relative the common monkeyflower (M. *guttatus*).

CHUPAROSA
Beloperone californica

Acanthus Family
Acanthaceae

This plant's common name translates from Spanish to mean "sucking rose," referring to its popularity with hummingbirds. The tubular red flowers (rarely yellow) appear in the spring on plants that can be over 6 feet (2 m) tall. Other birds, besides hummingbirds, are fond of chuparosa. Orioles, warblers, and goldfinches drink the nectar while quail and house finches eat the seeds. Look for this plant along low-elevation washes in March and April.

PINK TO PURPLE FLOWERS

Opposite: Arizona lupine (Lupinus arizonicus)

SAND VERBENA
Abronia villosa

Four-O'Clock Family
Nyctaginaceae

Following winters of abundant rainfall, thousands of visitors arrive to the sand dunes of the Colorado Desert to view the purple displays of this plant. In good years, sand verbena will carpet the wind-blown sands for several weeks in early spring with plants 1 to 3 feet across. The dunes of the Coachella Valley Preserve are a good place to enjoy these brief shows of color. Occasionally, plants with white flowers are found.

WINDMILLS
Allionia incarnata

Four-O'Clock Family
Nyctaginaceae

This prostrate perennial or winter annual gained its common name from its branches, which can radiate several feet from the center of the plant like a windmill. What appears to be a white- to rose-colored flower is really a cluster of three separate flowers. Windmills can be found on dry slopes and on dry sandy benches of the Colorado Desert.

FRINGED AMARANTH
Amaranthus fimbriatus

Amaranth Family
Amaranthaceae

Fringed amaranth is one of the ephemeral wildflowers found in the fall after summer rains. The plant grows erect to about 2 feet (60 cm) and the flowers are rose to lavender in color with fringes on their margins. Look for this plant at mid-elevations in dry sandy soils.

ROSE MALLOW
Sphaeralcea ambigua ssp. *rosacea*

Mallow Family
Malvaceae

Rose mallow is a sub-species of the more common desert or apricot mallow (see page 60). The flower color varies from a light pink to a dark rose. Rose mallow is found commonly at mid-elevations in the Santa Rosa Mountains and blooms in the spring.

DESERT FIVE-SPOT
Eremalche rotundifolia

Mallow Family
Malvaceae

Five-spot is one of the most elegant wildflowers found in the Colorado Desert. The rose-purple petals each have a large carmine spot at their base which gives the plant its common name. The plant is occasional to common on bajadas and in washes and grows to 16 inches (40 cm) or more tall. The flowers open in the afternoon and close up at night. A relative of desert five-spot is dune mallow (*Eremalche exilis*), a prostrate annual with white flowers that occurs on sand dunes.

DESERT HIBISCUS
Hibiscus denudatus

Mallow Family
Malvaceae

Desert hibiscus is a small shrub that grows to 2 feet (60 cm) tall and is found on bajadas and in washes throughout the desert southwest. In the western Colorado Desert it can be found on rocky slopes as well as bajadas. But, in the eastern desert it is mostly restricted to small, narrow washes that drain off desert pavements. The flowers are variable, ranging from white to pink. Looking at the leaves with a hand lens or other magnifier will reveal star-shaped hairs, characteristic of the family.

PINK FAIRY DUSTER
Calliandra eriophylla

Pea Family
Fabaceae

Fairy duster is an occasional perennial found in the Chocolate Mountains and east of the Colorado River in Arizona. This woody shrub grows to about 2 feet (60 cm) tall. The flowers are clustered, with long white to pink colored stamens. Fairy duster becomes more common in Arizona as an understory plant in saguaro forests.

ARIZONA LUPINE
Lupinus arizonicus

Pea Family
Fabaceae

Arizona lupine is a very common early spring ephemeral found throughout the Colorado Desert in loose soils. It can be especially abundant along the Interstate 10 freeway between Indio, California and Quartzite, Arizona. The flowers are purplish-pink with a yellow spot on the upper petal. This yellow spot will turn red after pollination, thereby discouraging insects from visiting flowers that have already been pollinated. Arizona lupine grows about 1 foot (30 cm) tall but can be twice that size in good years.

DESERT IRONWOOD
Olneya tesota

Pea Family
Fabaceae

Ironwood is a majestic tree that grows 25 feet (8 m) tall in washes of the Colorado Desert. The tree is appropriately named because the wood is dense enough to sink in water and is used extensively in Mexico for wood carvings. Rose-purple flowers appear in May and are followed by pods containing edible beans that taste like peanuts when roasted. Desert ironwood is one of several homes for the parasitic desert mistletoe (*Phoradendron californicum*) that commonly occurs on desert legumes.

COACHELLA VALLEY MILKVETCH
Astragalus lentiginosus var. *coachellae*

Pea Family
Fabaceae

Look for this rare spring ephemeral on the wind-blown sands of the Coachella Valley and nowhere else on earth. It is about 1 foot (30 cm) tall and bears purple flowers that turn blue after pollination by bees. The leaves are gray green and silky. Coachella Valley milkvetch is a member of a large plant group also known as locoweeds because some species accumulate the toxic metal selenium. Selenium causes "blind staggers" and death in cattle grazing on the plant. Several other species are known from the Colorado Desert.

SMOOTH-STEMMED FAGONIA
Fagonia laevis

Caltrop Family
Zygophyllaceae

This low, thin-stemmed plant is frequently missed because of its inconspicuous manner. Fagonia is an intricately branched plant usually less than 2 feet tall (60 cm) and has purple flowers. It is related to creosote bush, which is the most common native shrub in the Coachella Valley. Smooth-stemmed fagonia is common on dry rocky slopes.

DESERT HERON'S BILL
Erodium texanum

Heron's bill, an uncommon ephemeral with stems 4 to 16 inches (10 to 40 cm) long, is found on alluvial fans. It is related to common filaree (*E. cicutarium*), which is a weed in much of southern California. The two can be differentiated by their leaves, which are sort of fern-like in common filaree and clover-like in desert heron's bill.

CANCHALAGUA
Centaurium venustum

Gentian Family
Gentianaceae

Canchalagua is one of the few plants where the botanical name is easier to pronounce than the common name. Look for this rose-flowered annual along streams draining the Santa Rosa and San Jacinto mountains. Another similar member of the same genus is C. *exaltatum*, which has pale pink to white flowers with shorter petals. Both plants grow to over 1 foot (30 cm) tall. These wildflowers are more common on the coastal side of the mountains. Note that the stamens are spiraled like a corkscrew.

CATCHFLY GENTIAN
Eustoma exaltatum

Gentian Family
Gentianaceae

Catchfly gentian is a wonderful wildflower that starts blooming in late spring along almost every stream draining the Santa Rosa and San Jacinto mountains. The plant grows 1 to 2 feet (30 to 60 cm) tall and is a widespread wildflower found from one coast to the other.

BRISTLY GILIA
Langloisia setosissima

Phlox Family
Polemoniaceae

Several members of the genus *Langloisia* occur in the Colorado Desert, but only the flowers of bristly gilia are symmetrical and not two-lipped. This ephemeral is low and tufted with light violet flowers. The leaves are about 1 inch (25 mm) long and are edged with spines. Bristly gilia is locally frequent on bajadas and occasionally in sandy washes.

SCHOTT'S GILIA
Langloisia schottii

Schott's gilia is a common ephemeral 1 to 4 inches (2 to 10 cm) tall on gravelly or sandy bajadas throughout the Colorado Desert. The flowers are usually a light lavender, but can also be white, yellowish, or pinkish. A similiar plant is desert calico (*Langloisia matthewsii*). Schott's gilia has smaller flowers than desert calico, and the tips of the petals are pointed instead of squared.

BROAD-LEAFED GILIA
Gilia latifolia

Phlox Family
Polemoniaceae

Broad-leafed gilia, with its pink flowers and dark green leaves, is a desirable find at low elevations of the Colorado Desert. Look for this spring annual in the Mecca and Indio hills along the base of hot side canyons. Broad-leafed gilia is a small ephemeral to 12 inches (30 cm) tall, but usually less than half this size. The leaves are rounded and mostly located at the base of the flowering stalks.

NOTCH-LEAFED PHACELIA
Phacelia crenulata

Waterleaf Family
Hydrophyllaceae

Notched-leafed phacelia is a common ephemeral wildflower of the Colorado Desert. The plants are usually less than 12 inches (30 cm) tall, but can grow larger. The violet flowers are arranged into a tightly coiled scorpion-tail. The plant is ill-scented and the foliage is known to cause a rash similar to poison oak on some people. Look for this plant on bajadas and in sandy washes.

PURPLE MAT
Nama demissum

Waterleaf Family
Hydrophyllaceae

Purple mat is another of the ephemeral wildflowers commonly known as "belly flowers" because to see this plant it is necessary to get down on one's belly. The plant is small, about 3 inches (8 cm) wide, but in good years can form a mat 6 inches (15 cm) wide, literally covered with flowers. Purple mat can be found in the sandy soils of bajadas and washes.

CHIA
Salvia columbariae

Mint Family
Lamiaceae

Chia is a common spring wildflower in sandy, usually disturbed soils. The lavender to blue flowers are two lipped and congested into tight, prickly heads along narrow, square stems. Chia grows about 12 inches (30 cm) tall. The leaves are dark green, located at the base of the flower stalks, and smell a bit like skunk. Chia is the common name for several sages whose seeds were harvested by Native Americans for food.

DESERT MONKEYFLOWER
Mimulus bigelovii

Figwort Family
Scrophulariaceae

Desert monkeyflower is one of several monkeyflowers found in the Colorado Desert. The thin stems are topped with reddish purple flowers and grow to about 6 inches (15 cm) tall. Look for it in dry washes and on the sides of slopes. Areas in southern Anza-Borrego Desert State Park can have carpet displays of this wildflower.

SANTA ROSA BEARDTONGUE
Penstemon clevelandii ssp. *clevelandii*

Figwort Family
Scrophulariaceae

Santa Rosa beardtongue is a perennial found in washes of the southern mountains of Anza-Borrego Desert State Park. The flower stalks are about 2 feet (60 cm) long, and the flowers are red-purple, two-lipped, and about 1 inch (25 mm) long. Another sub-species, *P. clevlandii* ssp. *connatus*, is a rare plant found on rocky slopes of the Santa Rosa Mountains, and differs by having opposite pairs of leaves united at their base forming a disk around the stem.

BROOM-RAPE
Orobanche cooperi

Broom-Rape Family
Orobanchaceae

An unusual wildflower, broom-rape is a root parasite 4 to 12 inches (10 to 30 cm) tall on several desert species including creosote bush (*Larrea tridentata*), burro-bush (*Ambrosia dumosa*), and cheese bush (*Hymenoclea salsola*). The flowers are tubular with two lips and are congested into a dense spike. Since the plant is parasitic, the tissues lack chlorophyll and are purplish gray in color. This plant is relatively common, and over 30 plants can be clustered together in one location. It seems to prefer sandy soils.

DESERT WILLOW
Chilopsis linearis

Trumpet Creeper Family
Bignoniaceae

The large orchid-shaped flowers of desert willow are present from May until October and vary in color from white to lavender. The tree is common in desert washes and can be over 15 feet (5 m) tall. Desert willow is really not a willow at all and derives its common name from its willow-like leaves. This tree is one of the few in our desert that is winter deciduous, and it is a desirable landscape tree for a desert environment.

SPANISH NEEDLE
Palafoxia linearis

Sunflower Family
Asteraceae

Spanish needle is a common annual that blooms in both the spring and fall. Search for this plant along roadsides and washes where the soil has been disturbed. The plant grows to about 2 feet (60 cm) tall and the flowers are pink. Plants occurring near Yuma on the Imperial Dunes are the variety *gigantea*, which can grow to 6 feet (2 m) tall.

BORREGO ASTER
Machaeranthera orcuttii

Sunflower Family
Asteraceae

Borrego aster is a perennial wildflower 16 to 36 inches (40 to 90 cm) tall restricted to the Colorado Desert. It is locally abundant in the badland regions of Anza-Borrego Desert State Park. Two other asters also occur in the Colorado Desert—Mecca aster (*M. cognata*) and desert aster (*M. tortifolia*—see page 94). Mecca aster is mostly restricted to the Canebrake and Palm Springs geologic formations found in the Indio and Mecca hills. Desert aster is widespread on dry gravelly slopes and does not coexist with the other two.

DESERT ASTER
Machaeranthera tortifolia

Sunflower Family
Asteraceae

Desert aster is the most widespread of the three shrubby asters occurring in the Colorado Desert. The easiest method to tell the plants apart is location. If the plant is found in the Mecca Hills or the Borrego Badlands, it is most likely not desert aster. (See Borrego aster, page 93.) Desert aster is a shrub 12 to 28 inches (30 to 70 cm) tall found on gentle gravelly or rocky slopes and flats in any of the mountain ranges bordering the Chuckwalla Valley or Joshua Tree National Monument. This aster is definitely one of our nicest perennial desert wildflowers.

ANNUAL MITRA
Stephanomeria exigua

Sunflower Family
Asteraceae

Annual mitra is a common late season wildflower found on sand dunes. It grows to about 2 feet (60 cm) tall. The pink flowers appear as other dune wildflowers, like sand verbena and dune primrose, are starting to fade. Because the plant is light green and diffusely branched, it is possible to drive past this wildflower and never know it's there. A related perennial is desert straw (*S. pauciflora*), which is a small shrub found in washes.

BLUE FLOWERS

Opposite: Wild Heliotrope (Phacelia distans)

PARISH LARKSPUR
Delphinium parishii

This larkspur is occasionally found on sandy bajadas and in washes. It has a widespread distribution and is known from the northern Santa Rosa Mountains, Joshua Tree National Monument, the Chuckwalla Bench, and probably from other mid-elevation areas. The flower color varies from dark blue to lavender, sometimes with white. In spring, the flower stalk grows about 2 feet (60 cm) tall. The spur on the rear of the flower is characteristic.

SMOKE TREE
Dalea spinosa

Pea Family
Fabaceae

Smoke tree is a favorite among desert enthusiasts and grows abundantly in frost free washes of the Colorado Desert. It is a small tree that grows 3 to 20 feet (1 to 6 m) tall. The branches are mostly leafless, though leaves do appear for a short time in the spring. The flowers are dark blue and completely hide the tree for a few weeks in May or June. Smoke tree gets its common name from its growth habit and color, which make it look like a plume of smoke.

INDIGO BUSH
Dalea schottii

Pea Family
Fabaceae

Indigo bush is a dark blue flowered shrub that usually grows to 6 feet (2 m) tall, but can be taller. The leaves are narrow, unbranched, and about 1 inch (3 cm) long. It is common throughout the Colorado Desert in washes and on benches below 1,000 feet (300 m) elevation. A similar plant is California dalea (*Dalea californica*) which is found from the Whitewater area eastward to Twentynine Palms. California dalea differs by having narrow, branched leaves.

DESERT CANTERBURY BELLS
Phacelia campanularia

Waterleaf Family
Hydrophyllaceae

The large, deep blue, bell-shaped flowers and the rounded leaves are characteristic of the desert canterbury bell. This plant grows in dry sandy or gravelly soils such as in and along washes. Plants in protected areas can grow 2 feet (60 cm) tall, but normally canterbury bells is about half this size. A similar species (*P. parryi*) occurs along the western edge of the Colorado Desert but differs in having flowers that are slightly smaller and more open, instead of bell shaped. This plant, like notch-leafed phacelia, is known to cause a skin rash similar to poison oak in some people.

WILD HELIOTROPE
Phacelia distans

Waterleaf Family
Hydrophyllaceae

Wild heliotrope is an ephemeral shrub that generally grows up and through other shrubs. The flowers are light blue and about ¼ inch (6 mm) long. The fern-like leaves and the coiled, scorpion tail arrangement of the flowers are characteristic of this wildflower. In wet years the plant can grow quite large (2 feet, 60 cm) when supported by other shrubs.

SANTA ROSA SAGE
Salvia eremostachya

Mint Family
Lamiaceae

Santa Rosa sage is a perennial shrub with its distribution limited to rocky slopes below 3,000 feet (900 m) from the Santa Rosa Mountains near Palm Springs southward through the Peninsular Ranges into Baja California. The light blue flowers are strongly two lipped and arranged into heads along the flower stems. The plant is very woody, aromatic, and grows to about 2 feet (60 cm) or more tall. The leaves are about 1½ inches (35 mm) long and wrinkled above.

CACTUS FLOWERS

Opposite: Pencil Cholla (Opuntia ramosissima)

SILVER or GOLDEN CHOLLA
Opuntia echinocarpa

Cactus Family
Cactaceae

Silver or golden cholla is a highly variable cactus found throughout the Colorado Desert. The spines on the stems can be silver or golden, and the flowers are usually green but can age to dark red. It is relatively common on rocky flats and bajadas where it grows 2 to 4 feet (60 to 120 cm) tall. While similar to buckhorn cholla (facing page), the two are easy to tell apart. The bumps on the stem, called tubercles, are usually twice as long as wide in silver cholla, while the bumps on buckhorn cholla are three times longer than wide.

BUCKHORN CHOLLA
Opuntia acanthocarpa

Cactus Family
Cactaceae

Buckhorn cholla is a many-branched cane cactus that grows to 6 feet (2 m) tall in sandy or gravelly soils. The flowers are variable in color ranging from yellow to red. Silver cholla (*O. echinocarpa*—see facing page), a similar cholla found in the Colorado Desert, is often confused with buckhorn cholla. Silver cholla is generally smaller in size (3 feet, 1 m) with greenish to bronze colored flowers.

TEDDY-BEAR CHOLLA
Opuntia bigelovii

Cactus Family
Cactaceae

Teddy-bear cholla is commonly and inappropriately also called "jumping cholla." The stems, which are heavily covered with straw colored spines, readily detach from the parent but do not "jump" off the plant. An easy way to remove a piece of cholla if you should get stuck by one is to place a comb beneath the joint and launch it in an uninhabited direction. This cactus grows 2 to 5 feet (½ to 1½ m) tall, and its flowers are a light, clear yellow. Teddy-bear cholla is usually prolific on alluvial fans and benches, propagating itself from the joints that fall to the ground.

BEAVERTAIL CACTUS
Opuntia basilaris

An easy cactus to identify, beavertail lacks the long sharp spines commonly associated with cactus. Don't touch though, as the little dots that cover the pads contain very small spines called glochids, which can be hard to remove because of their small size (tape and tweezers work). The flowers are a brilliant magenta, making this cactus a favorite with wildflower photographers. The plant stays small, seldom growing over 1 foot (30 cm) tall.

MOJAVE MOUND, CLARET CUP

Echinocereus triglochidiatus

Cactus Family
Cactaceae

Mojave mound is a cactus that can form clumps up to 3 feet (1 m) wide and 1 foot (30 cm) tall. The plant occurs with Joshua trees or in pinyon-juniper woodlands in Joshua Tree National Monument, but can also be found in desert chaparral in Anza-Borrego Desert State Park. In spring the mounds can become covered with red to scarlet flowers that are visited by hummingbirds.

HEDGEHOG or CALICO CACTUS
Echinocereus engelmannii

The name calico cactus comes from the spines which can be multi-colored. Hedgehog is a columnar cactus growing to a little less than 1 foot (30 cm) tall in mounds of up to 15 or more stems. The flowers are a showy purplish red with yellow stamens and a green stigma rising from the center. This is a common cactus on rocky slopes and can sometimes be found on bajadas and in washes.

NIPPLE CACTUS
Mammillaria dioica

Cactus Family
Cactaceae

One look at the stem of this cactus and it is easy to see how it received its common name. The flowers are a creamy yellow with a colored mid-rib and are arranged on top of the stem in a ring. The plant is usually clumped and grows to 10 inches (25 cm). Nipple cactus has one to four dark central spines, but only one of them is hooked. Radial spines number 12 to 18 per nipple. A similar cactus, Graham nipple cactus (M. *microcarpa*), grows in the mountains along the Colorado River and eastward into Arizona. It differs in having more radial spines (18 to 28) per nipple.

CORKSEED CACTUS
Mammillaria tetrancistra

Corkseed is a cactus occasionally found growing beneath rocks or shrubs. This small cactus is usually about 4 inches (10 cm) tall, but plants 10 inches (25 cm) tall have been found. There are usually two to four central, hooked spines and 30 to 60 radial white spines which cover the body of the cactus. The flowers are white or pinkish with a rose colored mid-stripe and produce a scarlet fruit less than 1 inch (2 cm) long.

FOXTAIL CACTUS
Coryphantha vivipara var. *alversonii*

Foxtail cactus is a rare cactus of limited distribution in the mountains bordering the northern Colorado Desert. It is found from the Little San Bernardino Mountains in Joshua Tree National Monument to the Big Maria Mountains along the Colorado River. The plant differs from the nipple cacti by having a black tipped, unhooked central spine. The stems are usually clumped, but can be solitary and grow 8 inches (20 cm) tall. Flowers appear in late spring (May to June), and are pink with a darker mid-vein.

BARREL CACTUS, BISNAGA
Ferocactus acanthodes

Cactus Family
Cactaceae

California's second largest cactus is the barrel cactus (the largest is the saguaro). The stems of barrel cactus can grow to 9 feet (3 m), are usually solitary, but plants branched at the base are also known. The flowers are yellow with a red rib and produced in a ring at the top of the trunk. Against popular myth, lopping off the tops of these cacti will not produce life-sustaining water and only ruins the plant for life. Due to increased poaching, the plant is now fully protected in California and Arizona and cannot be removed legally from the wild.

INDEX